I0527914

Words
for
Building
Character

HS PRESS

Copyright © 2023 by Ryuho Okawa
English translation © Happy Science 2023
Original title: *Jinkaku o Tsukuru Kotoba*
HS Press is an imprint of IRH Press Co., Ltd.
Tokyo
ISBN: 979-8-88737-091-0
Cover Image: Mitsushi_Okada/amanaimages

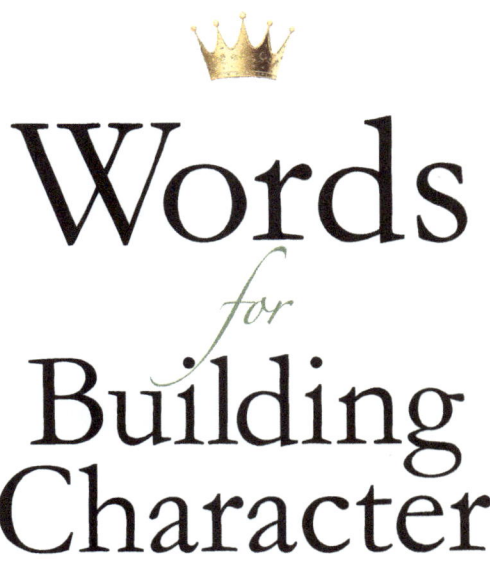

Words for Building Character

EL CANTARE

Ryuho Okawa

HS PRESS

Contents

Words for Building Character

Words for
Building Character

(1)

The starting point of love is not about asking for what you want.

②

If you fear that others will hurt

your ego, you have not yet

awaken to love.

(3)

Have you ever loved someone

until it hurts?

How empty a life is to always seek recognition from others.

(5)

How old do you need to be to

understand the phrase,

"A life of giving back"?

6

Gratitude is a joy that can be savored only by those who keep making effort.

(7)

Stay away from those who laugh at faith.

8

Those who have not awakened to

faith can never know the feeling:

"God is letting me live."

9

Do not praise yourself.

Rather, you should only praise

and glorify God.

Self-realization is
nothing but to live entirely
as God's hands and feet.

(11)

If you doubt God when faith

brings no benefit, you are

behaving like a mere animal.

12

Truly mediocre people are only
faithful when praised,
and immediately resentful
when reprimanded.

(13)

People who are always up

to no good when others are

not watching are the same as

untrained animals.

What is the false self?

You can compare it to a moth

that resembles a butterfly.

It is the side of you that

disappoints others when

they find it out.

(15)

Attractiveness is not about

how good you make yourself

appear but a light that naturally

shines out of your character.

Everyone is like an angel in times of success. Aim to be like an angel even in times of failure.

Truly beautiful are those who

do not lose faith in God

even in times of sadness.

18

Look within your mind.

If all you see is greed,

you have a long, long way to go.

In good times, we are happy.

But most of the time,

this happiness is temporary.

20

An ideal marriage is like
two streams meeting and
becoming a river.

(21)

One day, you will notice that

sexual love has become an illusion.

Even so, can you maintain peace

within yourself?

(22)

What is ugly appears beautiful,

and what is beautiful appears

ugly in your eyes.

This means you are still living in

the illusion of youth.

(23)

Children are not always adorable.

You were once like that too.

If you cannot feel your parents' love deeply, you have yet to become a decent human.

(25)

A warm and kind personality

cannot be made overnight.

(26)

A person who wishes to help
others will never go unnoticed
in the crowd.

Feel the Light of God in everything that has life.

(28)

Those who fall many times are also those who stand back up many times.

$\textcircled{29}$

Do not try to gain popularity

with a fake smile.

(30)

It is good to have a big dream

but remember,

reality is always tough.

(31)

It is true that cracked pearls are of no value. But still, do fake pearls look so beautiful to you?

(32)

A stone sinks in the pond

because it is heavy while oil floats

on the surface because it is light.

But who will be responsible for

the weight of your

worldly desires?

(33)

The more the ice, the more water it becomes. The many mistakes you make in life can be turned into many tools of wisdom for saving people.

(34)

In this world, people are more inclined to think that sexual desires are not sinful. But in the other world, the Hell of the Bloody Pond definitely exists.

(35)

Do not think that you own your
body. It is entrusted to you by
God and Buddha.

Make your body the vessel for

the holy spirit.

Heaven knows, earth knows,

you know, others know.

Wrongdoing will always be known.

Forgiving others' sins is the
practice of love.

(39)

When you feel like

judging others, tell yourself,

"Let he who is without sin,

cast the first stone."

40

Curses, spells, selfish desires,

and the tendency to exclude others

are the root causes of

becoming evil spirits.

If you often experience spiritual

phenomena, do not solely work

on spiritual matters but also

keep polishing your character.

(42)

There is the Law of Same Wavelength. When possession occurs, the possessing spirit and the possessed person are emitting the same wavelength.

High spirits will never come down to those with abnormality in judgment or behavior.

Therefore, correct yourself.
That is also the way to protect
yourself in the truest sense.

If you always hear a voice

that fuels your desires,

it is most likely

the voice of an evil spirit.

A person's academic background
does not reflect their spiritual level.
Sometimes, the more greedy
a person is, the more likely
they are to outdo their rivals.

High spirits are hidden among people who seem simple and foolish at first.

To see God, having a pure heart

is the first condition.

When a spirit comes to you and

claims to be a renowned figure,

you must calmly assess it,

be humble, and be objective.

(50)

Be rooted firmly to the ground like a big tree. Withstand any wind or rain, no matter what.

51

Your character will be reflected
in all aspects of handling money—
how you earn, use, manage,
and invest it.

Those who believe that money is the most important thing in this world will be shocked to find out that money is not used in the other world.

(53)

There must be nothing illegal or immoral in the way you get your income or raise funds.

Do not use money for

evil purposes.

Do not ruin people's lives

with money.

Attracting the opposite sex with money is a behavior you should be ashamed of.

Do not ruin people's lives
by making them addicted to
alcohol, narcotics, stimulants,
or illegal drugs and driving them
to become slaves to money.

However, it is an act of goodness and virtue to save money and accumulate wealth through honest and diligent work.

Use the money you gained

through honest means for

your self-improvement,

independence,

and responsible freedom.

(60)

Being stingy and saving money

are different.

These characteristics

will show in your face;

the former will make you look

mean while the latter will make

you look happy and wealthy.

61

Being willing to

share your happiness is

a precious mindset to have.

Be happy to share what you have.

People easily become corrupt

when they receive undeserved

recognition and get paid

too much for it.

(63)

Even those who work in the

priesthood, must have a virtuous

character and the diligence worthy

of receiving offerings.

For those who have excessive desires, having a tremendous amount of money is like living with a poisonous snake.

In running a business,

money is like blood;

aim to have good circulation and

create a virtuous circle.

Know that the amount of money

each person can handle depends

on their capacity.

If you are in a position to manage people, distribute profit with a fair and selfless mind.

68

A part of your money should be saved (Happiness Saving), shared (Happiness Sharing), and invested for the future (Happiness Planting).

The idea of storing wealth in heaven is neither heresy nor a wrong teaching; neither is it a consumer contract.

Some lawyers, politicians, and journalists think people can sue and demand a refund for the donations they made to religions. However, in the other world, they will be the ones judged by the Special Judge of Hell, Yama.

A man who becomes cold to his wife after marriage is like a fisherman who doesn't feed his catch. He is very poor in heart.

(72)

Men and women are equal in terms of their Buddha-nature, but they must be treated fairly as each gender has its missions and roles in this world.

Life is finite. So, live each day
to the fullest.

Even a parent and child have different souls. This is true in both a good and a bad way.

The problem with Japanese Shinto is that not only does it enshrine powerful figures in this world as gods, but it also enshrines those who died full of vengeance.

The other world is made fair by God, so do not think everyone is equal there.

Sadly, some people will fall to the Hell of Beasts, and be born as animals in the next life.

When necessary, God gives divine punishment to protect the third dimensional Earth as a training ground for souls.

(79)

Find life's purpose and mission.
They are the reason you are
living now.

The Earth must fulfill its
mission as the training ground
for the souls of space people too.

(81)

Death comes unexpectedly.
Whether you are a child or a
youth, always be prepared for it.

(82)

If you end up believing in atheism or materialism after soul training in this world, your life this time is a failure.

If you get divorced or remarried,
think of it as a new learning
environment.

Experience makes people learn
and become a little wiser.

Your body is given by God and your parents, so don't be reckless with it. Take good care of your body, and it will stay healthy and serve you long.

Strengthening your self-control

is the road to becoming an angel

or bodhisattva.

Self-control will be first tested

in youth when you have a

relationship with the

opposite sex.

Those who continue to refine themselves daily even in their old age will begin to emit the light of a halo.

Use studying as a way to
refine and cultivate your
mind and spirit.

90

In silence, store up the

wisdom of life

like honey.

$\boxed{91}$

During the trials of hell, know
that self-reflection and gratitude
are what you can rely on.

You will eventually have to leave this world. Remember this, and lessen your worldly attachments day by day.

(93)

As long as you have worldly desires, you cannot escape reincarnating between the Realms of Desire.

Buddha and Jesus are always there; you just haven't opened your eyes to the Truth.

Be in a state of mind where
you can look forward to the day
when you return to the
other world.

Out of all the attachments,

conceit and desire for fame are

the toughest to remove.

Those who have fully controlled their minds will proceed to the road to Buddha.

Faith is like getting your head above water and taking in air.

Do not think you are a "god"

so easily. Reflect on your

animalistic desires once again.

Think about the closing words

for the story of your life.

Afterword and Commentary

Following the two preceding publications of *Words for Life* and *Words for Work*, I have written a third book, *Words for Building Character*. It contains phrases that teach more about religious enlightenment.

There are many things I want to tell people, but since it is very hard to hold large seminars or lectures during the coronavirus pandemic, I have been expressing what I am thinking about through these 100 phrases of wisdom. Perhaps, many people will find it easier to learn the teachings this way. I hope our members will hold study sessions at their local temples or shojas when the opportunities arise.

These are short phrases, so if they are translated, I am sure our members around the world will also be able to grasp the main points of my philosophy with ease.

This book is a collaborative work of Jesus Christ, Shakyamuni Buddha, and the core consciousness of El Cantare. (On a side note, the first book was inspired by

Shakyamuni Buddha, and the second was by the Buddhist monk Bodhisattva Gyoki [Tathagata].)

I hope you will savor this book deeply.

Ryuho Okawa
Master & CEO of Happy Science Group
December 17, 2022

ABOUT THE AUTHOR

Founder and CEO of Happy Science Group.

Ryuho Okawa was born on July 7th 1956, in Tokushima, Japan. After graduating from the University of Tokyo with a law degree, he joined a Tokyo-based trading house. While working at its New York headquarters, he studied international finance at the Graduate Center of the City University of New York. In 1981, he attained Great Enlightenment and became aware that he is El Cantare with a mission to bring salvation to all humankind.

In 1986, he established Happy Science. It now has members in 168 countries across the world, with more than 700 branches and temples as well as 10,000 missionary houses around the world.

He has given over 3,500 lectures (of which more than 150 are in English) and published over 3,100 books (of which more than 600 are Spiritual Interview Series), and many are translated into 41 languages. Along with *The Laws of the Sun* and *The Laws of Hell*, many of the books have become best sellers or million sellers. To date, Happy Science has produced 27 movies. The original story and original concept were given by the Executive Producer Ryuho Okawa. He has also composed music and written lyrics of over 450 pieces.

Moreover, he is the Founder of Happy Science University and Happy Science Academy (Junior and Senior High School), Founder and President of the Happiness Realization Party, Founder and Honorary Headmaster of Happy Science Institute of Government and Management, Founder of IRH Press Co., Ltd., and the Chairperson of NEW STAR PRODUCTION Co., Ltd. and ARI Production Co., Ltd.

BOOKS BY RYUHO OKAWA

WORDS OF WISDOM SERIES

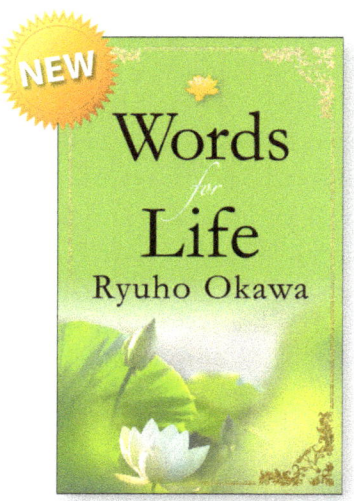

Words for Life

Paperback • 136 pages • $15.95
ISBN: 979-8-88727-089-7 (Mar. 16, 2023)

"I hope you'd take some time to flip through this book on the train, bus, or before you go to sleep, and meditate on the phrases and reflect on yourself."   -From Afterword and Commentary

Ryuho Okawa has written over 3,100 books on various topics. To help readers find the teachings that are beneficial for them out of the extensive teachings, the author has written 100 phrases and put them together in this book. Inside you will find words of wisdom that will help you improve your mindset, change you into a more capable and insightful person, and lead you to live a meaningful and happy life.

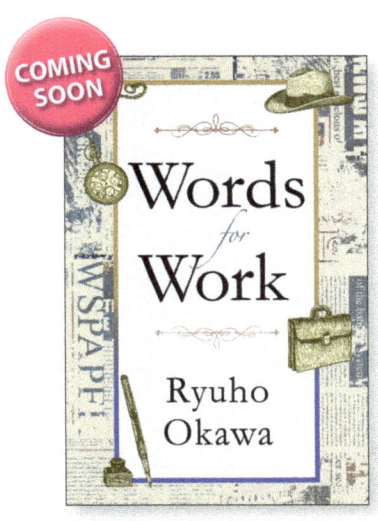

Words for Work

Paperback • 136 pages • $15.95
ISBN: 979-8-88737-090-3

To help readers find the teachings that are beneficial for them out of the extensive teachings, the author has published several books that compile 100 essential phrases. This book is the third English-translated book of the series.

Through his personal experiences at work and receiving inspiration from God and the angels in the heavenly world, Master Okawa has created these phrases regarding philosophies and practical wisdom about work. Have this book on your desk and it will be of great use to you throughout your career. Every day you can contemplate and gain tips on how to better your work as well as deepen your insight into company management.

El Cantare Trilogy

The Laws Series is an annual volume of books that are comprised of Ryuho Okawa's lectures that function as universal guidance to all people. They are of various topics that were given in accordance with the changes that each year brings. *The Laws of the Sun*, the first publication of the laws series, ranked in the annual best-selling list in Japan in 1994. Since, the laws series' titles have ranked in the annual best-selling list every year for more than two decades, setting socio-cultural trends in Japan and around the world.

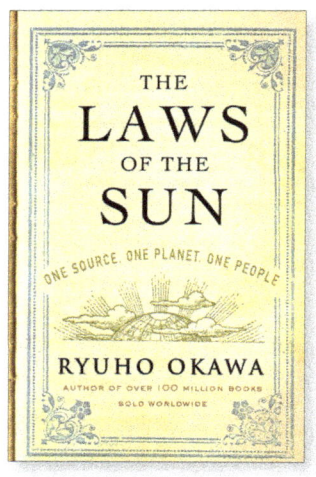

The Laws of the Sun

One Source, One Planet, One People

Paperback • 288 pages • $15.95
ISBN: 978-1-942125-43-3 (Oct. 15, 2018)

IMAGINE IF YOU COULD ASK GOD why He created this world and what spiritual laws He used to shape us—and everything around us. If we could understand His designs and intentions, we could discover what our goals in life should be and whether our actions move us closer to those goals or farther away.

At a young age, a spiritual calling prompted Ryuho Okawa to outline what he innately understood to be universal truths for all humankind. In *The Laws of the Sun*, Okawa outlines these laws of the universe and provides a road map for living one's life with greater purpose and meaning. In this powerful book, Ryuho Okawa reveals the transcendent nature of consciousness and the secrets of our multidimensional universe and our place in it. By understanding the different stages of love and following the Buddhist Eightfold Path, he believes we can speed up our eternal process of development. *The Laws of the Sun* shows the way to realize true happiness—a happiness that continues from this world through the other.

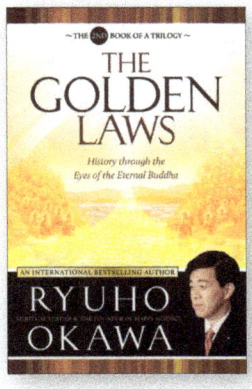

The Golden Laws

History through the Eyes of
the Eternal Buddha

E-book • 204 pages • $13.99
ISBN: 978-1-941779-82-8 (Sep. 24, 2015)

Throughout history, Great Guiding Spirits have been present on Earth in both the East and the West at crucial points in human history to further our spiritual development. *The Golden Laws* reveals how Divine Plan has been unfolding on Earth, and outlines 5,000 years of the secret history of humankind. Once we understand the true course of history, through past, present and into the future, we cannot help but become aware of the significance of our spiritual mission in the present age.

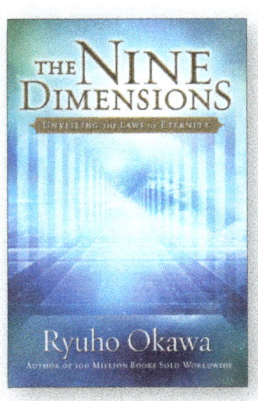

The Nine Dimensions

Unveiling the Laws of Eternity

Paperback • 168 pages • $15.95
ISBN: 978-0-982698-56-3 (Feb. 16, 2012)

This book is a window into the mind of our loving God, who designed this world and the vast, wondrous world of our afterlife as a school with many levels through which our souls learn and grow. When the religions and cultures of the world discover the truth of their common spiritual origin, they will be inspired to accept their differences, come together under faith in God, and build an era of harmony and peaceful progress on Earth.

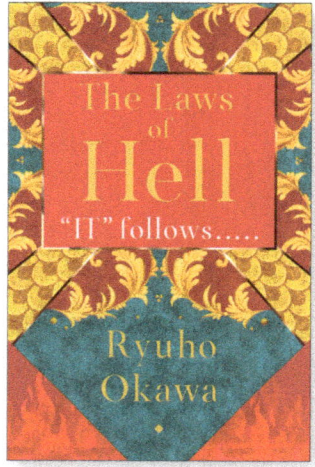

The Laws of Hell

"IT" follows .....

Paperback • 264 pages • $17.95
ISBN: 978-1-958655-04-7 (May 1, 2023)

Whether you believe it or not, the Spirit World and hell do exist. Currently, the Earth's population has exceeded 8 billion, and unfortunately, 1 in 2 people are falling to hell.

This book is a must-read at a time like this since more and more people are unknowingly heading to hell; the truth is, new areas of hell are being created, such as 'internet hell' and 'hell on earth.' Also, due to the widespread materialism, there is a sharp rise in the earthbound spirits wandering around Earth because they have no clue about the Spirit World.

To stop hell from spreading and to save the souls of all human beings, the Spiritual Master, Ryuho Okawa has compiled vital teachings in this book. This publication marks his 3,100th book and is the one and only comprehensive Truth about the modern hell.

New Books

The Road to Cultivate Yourself

Follow Your Silent Voice Within to Gain True Wisdom

Paperback • 256 pages • $17.95
ISBN: 978-1-958655-05-4 (Jun. 22, 2023)

What is the ideal way of living when chaos and destruction are accelerated?

This book offers unchanging Truth in the ever-changing world, such as the secrets to become more aware about the spiritual self and how to increase intellectual productivity amidst the rapid changes of the modern age. It is packed with Ryuho Okawa's crystalized wisdom of life.

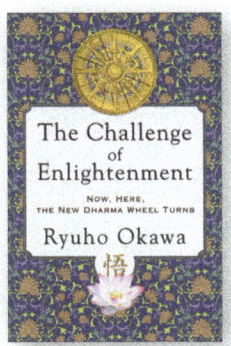

The Challenge of Enlightenment

Now, Here, the New Dharma Wheel Turns

Paperback • 380 pages • $17.95
ISBN: 978-1-942125-92-1 (Dec. 20, 2022)

Buddha's teachings, a reflection of his eternal wisdom, are like a bamboo pole used to change the course of your boat in the rapid stream of the great river called life. By reading this book, your mind becomes clearer, learns to savor inner peace, and it will empower you to make profound life improvements.

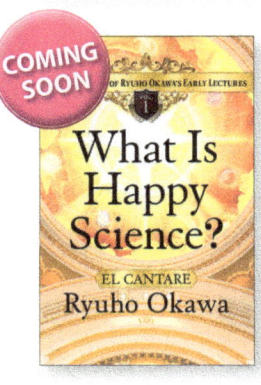

What Is Happy Science?

Best Selection of Ryuho Okawa's Early Lectures (Volume 1)

Paperback • 256 pages • $17.95
ISBN: 978-1-942125-99-0 (Aug. 25, 2023)

The Best Selection series is a collection of Ryuho Okawa's passionate lectures during the ages of 32 to 33 that reveal the mission and goal of Happy Science. This book contains the eternal Truth, including the meaning of life, the secret of the mind, the true meaning of love, the mystery of the universe, and how to end hatred and world conflicts.

Bestselling Buddhist Titles

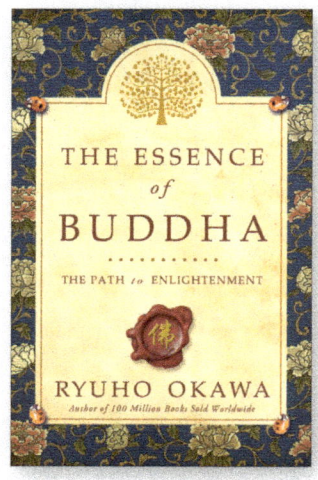

The Essence of Buddha

The Path to Enlightenment

Paperback • 208 pages • $14.95
ISBN: 978-1-942125-06-8 (Oct.1, 2016)

In this book, Ryuho Okawa imparts in simple and accessible language his wisdom about the essence of Shakyamuni Buddha's philosophy of life and enlightenment-teachings that have been inspiring people all over the world for over 2,500 years. By offering a new perspective on core Buddhist thoughts that have long been cloaked in mystique, Okawa brings these teachings to life for modern people. *The Essence of Buddha* distills a way of life that anyone can practice to achieve a life of self-growth, compassionate living, and true happiness.

The True Eightfold Path

Guideposts for Self-Innovation

Paperback • 256 pages • $16.95
ISBN: 978-1-942125-80-8 (Mar. 30, 2021)

This book explains how we can apply the Eightfold Path, one of the main pillars of Shakyamuni Buddha's teachings, as everyday guideposts in the modern-age to achieve self-innovation to live better and make positive changes in these uncertain times.

The Rebirth of Buddha

My Eternal Disciples, Hear My Words

Paperback • 280 pages • $17.95
ISBN: 978-1-942125-95-2 (Jul. 15, 2022)

These are the messages of Buddha who has returned to this modern age as promised to His eternal beloved disciples. They are in simple words and poetic style, yet contain profound messages. Once you start reading these passages, your soul will be replenished as the plant absorbs the water, and you will remember why you chose this era to be born into with Buddha. Listen to the voices of your Eternal Master and awaken to your calling.

Rojin, Buddha's Mystical Power

Its Ultimate Attainment in Today's World

Paperback • 224 pages • $16.95
ISBN: 978-1-942125-82-2 (Sep. 24, 2021)

In this book, Ryuho Okawa has redefined the traditional Buddhist term *Rojin* and explained that in modern society it means the following: the ability for individuals with great spiritual powers to live in the world as people with common sense while using their abilities to the optimal level. This book will unravel the mystery of the mind and lead you to the path to enlightenment.

The New Genre of Spiritual Mystery Novel
- The Unknown Stigma Trilogy -

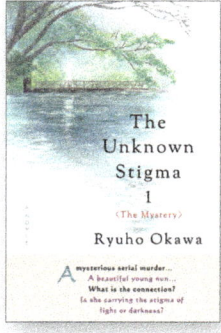

The Unknown Stigma 1 <The Mystery>

Hardcover • 192 pages • $17.95
ISBN: 978-1-942125-28-0 (Oct. 1, 2022)

The first spiritual mystery novel by Ryuho Okawa. It happened one early summer afternoon, in a densely wooded park in Tokyo: following a loud scream of a young woman, the alleged victim was found lying with his eyes rolled back and foaming at the mouth. But there was no sign of forced trauma, nor even a drop of blood. Then, similar murder cases continued one after another without any clues. Later, this mysterious serial murder case leads back to a young Catholic nun...

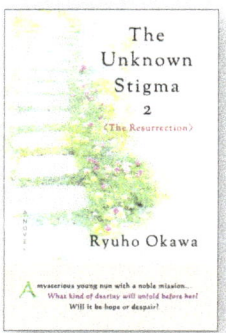

The Unknown Stigma 2 <The Resurrection>

Hardcover • 180 pages • $17.95
ISBN: 978-1-942125-31-0 (Nov. 1, 2022)

A sequel to *The Unknown Stigma 1 <The Mystery>* by Ryuho Okawa. After an extraordinary spiritual experience, a young, mysterious Catholic nun is now endowed with a new, noble mission. What kind of destiny will she face? Will it be hope or despair that awaits her? The story develops into a turn of events that no one could ever have anticipated. Are you ready to embrace its shocking ending?

The Unknown Stigma 3 <The Universe>

Hardcover • 184 pages • $17.95
ISBN: 978-1-958655-00-9 (Dec. 1, 2022)

In this astonishing sequel to the first two installments of *The Unknown Stigma*, the protagonist journeys through the universe and encounters a mystical world unknown to humankind. Discover what awaits her beyond this mysterious world.

Other Recommended Titles

The Ten Principles from El Cantare Volume I
Ryuho Okawa's First Lectures on His Basic Teachings

The Ten Principles from El Cantare Volume II
Ryuho Okawa's First Lectures on His Wish to Save the World

Twiceborn
My Early Thoughts that Revealed My True Mission

Developmental Stages of Love - The Original Theory
Philosophy of Love in My Youth

The Miracle of Meditation
Opening Your Life to Peace, Joy and the Power Within

The Laws of Secret
Awaken to This New World and Change Your Life

The Challenge of the Mind
An Essential Guide to Buddha's Teachings:
Zen, Karma and Enlightenment

The Power of Basics
Introduction to Modern Zen Life
of Calm, Spirituality and Success

Spiritual World 101
A guide to a spiritually happy life

For a complete list of books, visit <u>okawabooks.com</u>

WHO IS EL CANTARE?

El Cantare means "the Light of the Earth." He is the Supreme God of the Earth who has been guiding humankind since the beginning of Genesis, and He is the Creator of the universe. He is whom Jesus called Father and Muhammad called Allah, and is *Ame-no-Mioya-Gami*, Japanese Father God. Different parts of El Cantare's core consciousness have descended to Earth in the past, once as Alpha and another as Elohim. His branch spirits, such as Shakyamuni Buddha and Hermes, have descended to Earth many times and helped to flourish many civilizations. To unite various religions and to integrate various fields of study in order to build a new civilization on Earth, a part of the core consciousness has descended to Earth as Master Ryuho Okawa.

Alpha is a part of the core consciousness of El Cantare who descended to Earth around 330 million years ago. Alpha preached Earth's Truths to harmonize and unify Earth-born humans and space people who came from other planets.

Elohim is a part of the core consciousness of El Cantare who descended to Earth around 150 million years ago. He gave wisdom, mainly on the differences of light and darkness, good and evil.

Ame-no-Mioya-Gami (Japanese Father God) is the Creator God and the Father God who appears in the ancient literature, *Hotsuma Tsutae.* It is believed that He descended on the foothills of Mt. Fuji about 30,000 years ago and built the Fuji dynasty, which is the root of the Japanese civilization. With justice as the central pillar, Ame-no-Mioya-Gami's teachings spread to ancient civilizations of other countries in the world.

Shakyamuni Buddha was born as a prince into the Shakya Clan in India around 2,600 years ago. When he was 29 years old, he renounced the world and sought enlightenment. He later attained Great Enlightenment and founded Buddhism.

Hermes is one of the 12 Olympian gods in Greek mythology, but the spiritual Truth is that he taught the teachings of love and progress around 4,300 years ago that became the origin of the current Western civilization. He is a hero that truly existed.

Ophealis was born in Greece around 6,500 years ago and was the leader who took an expedition to as far as Egypt. He is the God of miracles, prosperity, and arts, and is known as Osiris in the Egyptian mythology.

Rient Arl Croud was born as a king of the ancient Incan Empire around 7,000 years ago and taught about the mysteries of the mind. In the heavenly world, he is responsible for the interactions that take place between various planets.

Thoth was an almighty leader who built the golden age of the Atlantic civilization around 12,000 years ago. In the Egyptian mythology, he is known as God Thoth.

Ra Mu was a leader who built the golden age of the civilization of Mu around 17,000 years ago. As a religious leader and a politician, he ruled by uniting religion and politics.

ABOUT HAPPY SCIENCE

Happy Science is a religious group founded on the faith in El Cantare who is the God of the Earth, and the Creator of the universe. The essence of human beings is the soul that was created by God, and we all are children of God. God is our true parent, so in our souls we have a fundamental desire to "believe in God, love God, and get closer to God." And, we can get closer to God by living with God's Will as our own. In Happy Science, we call this the "Exploration of Right Mind." More specifically, it means to practice the Fourfold Path, which consists of "Love, Wisdom, Self-Reflection, and Progress."

Love: Love means "love that gives," or mercy. God hopes for the happiness of all people. Therefore, living with God's Will as our own means to start by practicing "love that gives."

Wisdom: God's love is boundless. It is important to learn various Truths in order to understand the heart of God.

Self-Reflection: Once you learn the heart of God and the difference between His mind and yours, you should strive to bring your own mind closer to the mind of God—that process is called self-reflection. Self-reflection also includes meditation and prayer.

Progress: Since God hopes for the happiness of all people, you should also make progress in your love, and make an effort to realize utopia in which everyone in your society, country, and eventually all humankind can become happy.

As we practice this Fourfold Path, our souls will advance toward God step by step. That is when we can attain real happiness—our souls' desire to get closer to God comes true.

In Happy Science, we conduct activities to make ourselves happy through belief in Lord El Cantare, and to spread this faith to the world and bring happiness to all. We welcome you to join our activities!

We hold events and activities to help you practice the Fourfold Path at our branches, temples, missionary centers and missionary houses

Love: We hold various volunteering activities. Our members conduct missionary work together as the greatest practice of love.

Wisdom: We offer our comprehensive books collection, many of which bookstores do not have available. In addition, we give out numerous opportunities such as seminars or book clubs to learn the Truth.

Self-Reflection: We offer opportunities to polish your mind through self-reflection, meditation, and prayer. There are many cases in which members have experienced improvement in their human relationships by changing their own minds.

Progress: We also offer seminars to enhance your power of influence. Because it is also important to do well at work to make society better, we hold seminars to improve your work and management skills.

HAPPY SCIENCE'S ENGLISH SUTRA

"The True Words Spoken By Buddha"

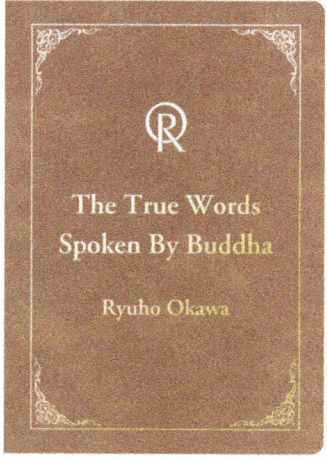

The True Words Spoken By Buddha is an English sutra given directly from the spirit of Shakyamuni Buddha, who is a part of Master Ryuho Okawa's subconscious. The words in this sutra are not of a mere human being but are the words of God or Buddha sent directly from the ninth dimension, which is the highest realm of the Earth's Spirit World.

The True Words Spoken By Buddha is an essential sutra for us to connect and live with God or Buddha's Will as our own.

MEMBERSHIPS

MEMBERSHIP

If you would like to know more about Happy Science, please consider becoming a member. Those who pledge to believe in Lord El Cantare and wish to learn more can join us.

When you become a member, you will receive the following sutra books: *The True Words Spoken By Buddha*, *Prayer to the Lord* and *Prayer to Guardian and Guiding Spirits*.

DEVOTEE MEMBER

If you would like to learn the teachings of Happy Science and walk the path of faith, become a Devotee member who pledges devotion to the Three Treasures, which are Buddha, Dharma, and Sangha. Buddha refers to Lord El Cantare, Master Ryuho Okawa. Dharma refers to Master Ryuho Okawa's teachings. Sangha refers to Happy Science. Devoting to the Three Treasures will let your Buddha-nature shine, and you will enter the path to attain true freedom of the mind.

Becoming a devotee means you become Buddha's disciple. You will discipline your mind and act to bring happiness to society.

✉ **EMAIL** or ☎ **PHONE CALL**
Please see the contact information page.

📶 **ONLINE**   member.happy-science.org/signup/ 🔍

CONTACT INFORMATION

Happy Science is a worldwide organization with branches and temples around the globe. For a comprehensive list, visit the worldwide directory at happy-science.org. The following are some of our main Happy Science locations:

UNITED STATES AND CANADA

New York
79 Franklin St., New York, NY 10013, USA
Phone: 1-212-343-7972
Fax: 1-212-343-7973
Email: ny@happy-science.org
Website: happyscience-usa.org

New Jersey
66 Hudson St., #2R, Hoboken, NJ 07030, USA
Phone: 1-201-313-0127
Email: nj@happy-science.org
Website: happyscience-usa.org

Chicago
2300 Barrington Rd., Suite #400,
Hoffman Estates, IL 60169, USA
Phone: 1-630-937-3077
Email: chicago@happy-science.org
Website: happyscience-usa.org

Florida
5208 8th St., Zephyrhills, FL 33542, USA
Phone: 1-813-715-0000
Fax: 1-813-715-0010
Email: florida@happy-science.org
Website: happyscience-usa.org

Atlanta
1874 Piedmont Ave., NE Suite 360-C
Atlanta, GA 30324, USA
Phone: 1-404-892-7770
Email: atlanta@happy-science.org
Website: happyscience-usa.org

San Francisco
525 Clinton St.
Redwood City, CA 94062, USA
Phone & Fax: 1-650-363-2777
Email: sf@happy-science.org
Website: happyscience-usa.org

Los Angeles
1590 E. Del Mar Blvd., Pasadena, CA
91106, USA
Phone: 1-626-395-7775
Fax: 1-626-395-7776
Email: la@happy-science.org
Website: happyscience-usa.org

Orange County
16541 Gothard St. Suite 104
Huntington Beach, CA 92647
Phone: 1-714-659-1501
Email: oc@happy-science.org
Website: happyscience-usa.org

San Diego
7841 Balboa Ave. Suite #202
San Diego, CA 92111, USA
Phone: 1-626-395-7775
Fax: 1-626-395-7776
E-mail: sandiego@happy-science.org
Website: happyscience-usa.org

Hawaii
Phone: 1-808-591-9772
Fax: 1-808-591-9776
Email: hi@happy-science.org
Website: happyscience-usa.org

Kauai
3343 Kanakolu Street, Suite 5
Lihue, HI 96766, USA
Phone: 1-808-822-7007
Fax: 1-808-822-6007
Email: kauai-hi@happy-science.org
Website: happyscience-usa.org

Toronto

845 The Queensway
Etobicoke, ON M8Z 1N6, Canada
Phone: 1-416-901-3747
Email: toronto@happy-science.org
Website: happy-science.ca

Vancouver

#201-2607 East 49th Avenue,
Vancouver, BC, V5S 1J9, Canada
Phone: 1-604-437-7735
Fax: 1-604-437-7764
Email: vancouver@happy-science.org
Website: happy-science.ca

INTERNATIONAL

Tokyo

1-6-7 Togoshi, Shinagawa,
Tokyo, 142-0041, Japan
Phone: 81-3-6384-5770
Fax: 81-3-6384-5776
Email: tokyo@happy-science.org
Website: happy-science.org

London

3 Margaret St.
London, W1W 8RE United Kingdom
Phone: 44-20-7323-9255
Fax: 44-20-7323-9344
Email: eu@happy-science.org
Website: www.happyscience-uk.org

Sydney

516 Pacific Highway, Lane Cove North,
2066 NSW, Australia
Phone: 61-2-9411-2877
Fax: 61-2-9411-2822
Email: sydney@happy-science.org

Sao Paulo

Rua. Domingos de Morais 1154,
Vila Mariana, Sao Paulo SP
CEP 04010-100, Brazil
Phone: 55-11-5088-3800
Email: sp@happy-science.org
Website: happyscience.com.br

Jundiai

Rua Congo, 447, Jd. Bonfiglioli
Jundiai-CEP, 13207-340, Brazil
Phone: 55-11-4587-5952
Email: jundiai@happy-science.org

Seoul

74, Sadang-ro 27-gil,
Dongjak-gu, Seoul, Korea
Phone: 82-2-3478-8777
Fax: 82-2-3478-9777
Email: korea@happy-science.org

Taipei

No. 89, Lane 155, Dunhua N. Road,
Songshan District, Taipei City 105, Taiwan
Phone: 886-2-2719-9377
Fax: 886-2-2719-5570
Email: taiwan@happy-science.org

Taichung

No. 146, Minzu Rd., Central Dist.,
Taichung City 400001, Taiwan (R.O.C.)
Phone: 886-4-22233777
Email: taichung@happy-science.org

Kuala Lumpur

No 22A, Block 2, Jalil Link Jalan Jalil
Jaya 2, Bukit Jalil 57000,
Kuala Lumpur, Malaysia
Phone: 60-3-8998-7877
Fax: 60-3-8998-7977
Email: malaysia@happy-science.org
Website: happyscience.org.my

Kathmandu

Kathmandu Metropolitan City,
Ward No. 15, Ring Road, Kimdol,
Sitapaila Kathmandu, Nepal
Phone: 977-1-537-2931
Email: nepal@happy-science.org

Kampala

Plot 877 Rubaga Road, Kampala
P.O. Box 34130 Kampala, UGANDA
Email: uganda@happy-science.org

The Happiness Realization Party (HRP) was founded in May 2009 by Master Ryuho Okawa as part of the Happy Science Group. HRP strives to improve the Japanese society, based on three basic political principles of "freedom, democracy, and faith," and let Japan promote individual and public happiness from Asia to the world as a leader nation.

1) Diplomacy and Security: Protecting Freedom, Democracy, and Faith of Japan and the World from China's Totalitarianism

Japan's current defense system is insufficient against China's expanding hegemony and the threat of North Korea's nuclear missiles. Japan, as the leader of Asia, must strengthen its defense power and promote strategic diplomacy together with the nations which share the values of freedom, democracy, and faith. Further, HRP aims to realize world peace under the leadership of Japan, the nation with the spirit of religious tolerance.

2) Economy: Early economic recovery through utilizing the "wisdom of the private sector"

Economy has been damaged severely by the novel coronavirus originated in China. Many companies have been forced into bankruptcy or out of business. What is needed for economic recovery now is not subsidies and regulations by the government, but policies which can utilize the "wisdom of the private sector."

For more information, visit en.hr-party.jp

HAPPY SCIENCE ACADEMY JUNIOR AND SENIOR HIGH SCHOOL

Happy Science Academy Junior and Senior High School is a boarding school founded with the goal of educating the future leaders of the world who can have a big vision, persevere, and take on new challenges.

Currently, there are two campuses in Japan; the Nasu Main Campus in Tochigi Prefecture, founded in 2010, and the Kansai Campus in Shiga Prefecture, founded in 2013.

 # HAPPY SCIENCE UNIVERSITY

THE FOUNDING SPIRIT AND THE GOAL OF EDUCATION

Based on the founding philosophy of the university, "Exploration of happiness and the creation of a new civilization," education, research and studies will be provided to help students acquire deep understanding grounded in religious belief and advanced expertise with the objectives of producing "great talents of virtue" who can contribute in a broad-ranging way to serving Japan and the international society.

ABOUT HS PRESS

HS Press is an imprint of IRH Press Co., Ltd. IRH Press Co., Ltd., based in Tokyo, was founded in 1987 as a publishing division of Happy Science. IRH Press publishes religious and spiritual books, journals, magazines and also operates broadcast and film production enterprises. For more information, visit *okawabooks.com*.

Follow us on:

f Facebook: Okawa Books   ◉ Instagram: OkawaBooks

▶ Youtube: Okawa Books   🐦 Twitter: Okawa Books

𝓟 Pinterest: Okawa Books   g Goodreads: Ryuho Okawa

──────── **NEWSLETTER** ────────

To receive book related news, promotions and events, please subscribe to our newsletter below.

∅ irhpress.com/pages/subscribe

 ──────── **AUDIO / VISUAL MEDIA** ────────

YOUTUBE

PODCAST

Introduction of Ryuho Okawa's titles; topics ranging from self-help, current affairs, spirituality, religion, and the universe.

www.ingramcontent.com/pod-product-compliance
Lightning Source LLC
Chambersburg PA
CBHW051317120626
46547CB00015B/2282